Do Jellyfish Like Peanut Butter?

Amazing Sea Creature Facts

PERSNICKETY PRESS

Design by Shan Stumpf

ISBN: 978-1-943978-44-1

10 9 8 7 6 5 4 3 2 1

Printed in United States of America

CPSIA tracking label information
Production Location: CG Book Printers
North Mankato, Minnesota
Production Date: February 2020
Cohort: Batch No. 294306

For Demetria, Ariadne,
Devon, Morgan, and all
kids who love the sea.
— A.R. & C.D.

PERSNICKETY PRESS

Produced by Persnickety Press
120A North Salem Street
Apex, NC 27502

WunderMill
WunderMillBooks.com

Do Jellyfish Like Peanut Butter?

Amazing Sea Creature Facts

By Corinne Demas &
Artemis Roehrig

Illustrated by Ellen Shi

Do starfish sign autographs?

No! But they use their finger-like arms to pry open clams, oysters, and other mollusks that they want to eat.

Do trumpet fish play in marching bands?

No! But they swim vertically to camouflage themselves in the seaweed. This makes them look as if they're marching.

Do seahorses wear saddles?

No! But male seahorses have a pouch on the front of their tail where they carry the females' eggs until they're ready to hatch.

Do lampreys get plugged in?

No! But they prey on fish by attaching their mouths to a fish's body and sucking out the blood.

Do clownfish perform at the circus?

No! But they do a lively dance around the tentacles of the sea anemone they live with.

Do pilot whales hang out in airports?

No! But they hang out with other pilot whales in groups of ten to one hundred called "pods." Different pods get together for mating and protection.

Do football fish catch passes?

No! But they catch prey with the help of a glowing lure on what looks like a fishing rod at the top of their head.

Do mussels work out at the gym?

No! But using strong, sticky threads, they attach themselves to rocks, so even big waves can't wash them away.

Do skates slide across the ice?

No! But they glide along the ocean floor by rippling their fins.

Do hammerhead sharks build houses?

No! But they use their hammer-shaped heads to hold down stingrays while they eat them.

Do jellyfish like peanut butter?

No! But their bodies are made of a jelly-like substance. Although they're called jellyfish, they have no bones and actually aren't fish at all. They're 95% water! (But don't drink one if you're thirsty...)

Do sea lions roar?

YES!

They roar to protect their territory and when they feel threatened. The males in two species of large sea lions even have manes!

WHAT'S IN THE SEA ?

The sea is filled with a wonderful variety of animals—tiny, huge, and everything in between. Mammals (like pilot whales and sea lions) and fish (like trumpet fish, clownfish, football fish, sea horses, lampreys, skates, and hammerhead sharks) are all vertebrates (animals with backbones). Jellyfish, mussels, and starfish are all invertebrates (animals without backbones). All of these animals play an important role in maintaining the fragile balance of life in the ocean.

Scientists who study sea creatures are called marine biologists. The survival of many sea creatures is at risk due to climate change, overfishing, pollution, and plastic trash. Currently, less than 5% of the world's oceans are marine protected areas.

STARFISH
(Class: Asteroidea)

A more accurate name for starfish is "sea stars," as they are not actually fish at all—they are more closely related to sand dollars and sea urchins. There are over 2,000 different species of starfish! Most have five arms, but some species have more. One species even has 40 arms! If an arm is broken off, they can grow it back, but this can take a long time. Starfish have a stomach on the bottom of their body, but no brain. They can live to be 35 years old.

TRUMPET FISH
(Genus: Aulostomus)

Trumpet Fish are about three feet long with a very skinny body. They eat little fish and invertebrates, which they suck into their mouth, just like sucking through a straw. Another name for them is the Flutemouth. There are three different species, all of which live in tropical water, usually in reefs.

SEAHORSES
(Genus: Hippocampus)

There are 45 species of seahorses. Seahorses are unique because the female transfers her eggs to a pouch on the male seahorse, where they develop into babies. Seahorses are threatened by humans, who kill them for use in traditional medicine, dry them to sell as souvenirs, and capture them for sale as pets.

LAMPREYS
(Order: Petromyzontiformes)

There are 38 different species of lampreys. They are about 12 to 20 inches long. They are parasitic, which means they attach themselves onto their prey and then eat while staying attached for as long as several weeks. Their mouth is shaped like a funnel with teeth. Lampreys aren't entirely sea creatures, since they are born in fresh water and then migrate to oceans as adults. Some species remain in fresh water their entire lives.

CLOWNFISH
(Family: Amphiprioninae)

Clownfish are also known as anemonefish since they live with anemones. Clownfish clean the anemones, and the anemones—which have venomous tentacles—protect the clownfish from predators. Scientists think that clownfish are protected from the stings either by the mucus coating on their bodies, or because they slowly acclimate themselves to the venom. All clownfish are born male, and some later change into females. Clownfish live in the Indian Ocean, Red Sea, and Western Pacific Ocean.

PILOT WHALES
(Genus: Globicephala)

There are two different species of pilot whales—the long-finned pilot whale and the short-finned pilot whale. Despite their name, they are actually a type of dolphin and are sometimes called black-fish, which is equally confusing since they aren't fish at all—they're mammals! Male pilot whales can reach 25 feet in length and weigh up to 5,000 pounds. Their diet includes squid and fish.

FOOTBALL FISH
(Family: Himantolophidae)

There are 22 different species of football fish, which are a type of anglerfish. The much-smaller males attach themselves to the females and become parasites, getting their nutrients straight from the females' bodies. The spine that looks like a fishing rod coming off their head is called an illicium. The "lure" is called an esca, and the glow comes from bioluminescent bacteria. The glow attracts prey in the deep parts of the ocean where there is no light.

MUSSELS
(Family: Mytilidae)

Mussels are bivalves, which means they have two shells that are attached with a hinge. There are families of mussels that live in fresh water and others that live in salt water, which are the ones people eat. There are 17 different species of mussels that are considered edible by humans. Mussels eat by sucking water in through their siphon and straining out the plankton for food.

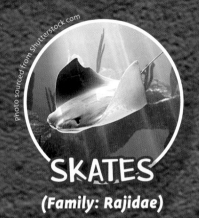

SKATES
(Family: Rajidae)

There are 150 different species of skates. They are often confused with sting rays, but sting rays have live births, and skates lay eggs. A skate egg case looks like a pouch and is often called a "mermaid's purse." Skates' mouths are on the underside of their bodies, and they glide around on the ocean floor searching for food such as shrimp, crabs, and mollusks. Their fluid-like movement is called rajiform locomotion.

JELLYFISH
(Subphylum: Medusozoa)

Jellyfish are sometimes called sea jellies, since they are not actually fish and are more closely related to coral and anemones. There are about 4,000 different species of jellyfish. One species of jellyfish, called the lion's mane, can have tentacles up to 120 feet long. Jellyfish tentacles have stingers, called nematocysts, that are used for defense and to help capture prey.

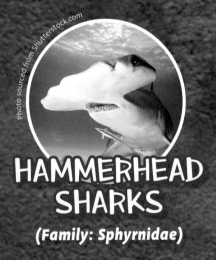

HAMMERHEAD SHARKS
(Family: Sphyrnidae)

There are nine different species of hammerhead sharks. The hammer shape on their head is called a cephalofoil. Their eyes are far apart, so they can see almost 360 degrees around their body. They are carnivores and eat fish, octopuses, crabs, and sometimes even other hammerhead sharks! They live between 25 and 35 years. During the summer, they migrate from the tropics to colder water. They can be almost 20 feet long and weigh 1,200 pounds. Some species of hammerhead sharks are endangered because of overfishing.

SEA LIONS
(Subfamily: Otariinae)

Sea lions are mammals and live for 20 to 30 years. The largest species of sea lion weighs 2,200 pounds and is six feet long. Sea lions are sometimes kept in captivity because they can be trained to do tricks in aquariums and circuses and to do work for the Navy. Unlike seals, sea lions have visible ear flaps and can "walk" on their flippers.